Dad's Storybook

wisdom, wit, and words of advice

Plain Sight Publishing
an Imprint of Cedar Fort, Inc.
Springville, Utah

ISBN 13: 978-1-4621-1803-8

Published by Plain Sight Publishing, an imprint of Cedar Fort, Inc.
2373 W. 700 S., Springville, UT 84663
Distributed by Cedar Fort, Inc., www.cedarfort.com

Library of Congress Control Number: 2015955448

Cover design by Lauren Error
Page design by Krystal Wares
Cover design © 2016 by Cedar Fort, Inc.
Edited by Rebecca Bird

Printed in China

10 9 8 7 6 5 4 3

Printed on acid-free paper

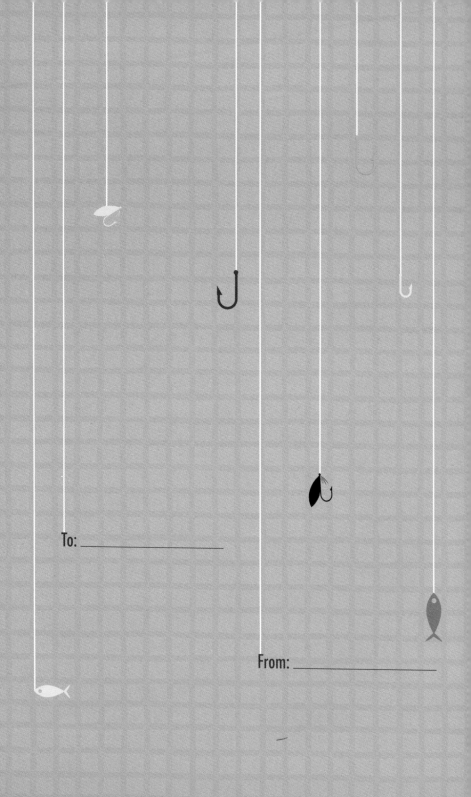

To: _____

From: _____

Table of Contents

Introduction 1

Family Stories 7

Family Traditions 15

Activity: The Dad Treasure Hunt 21

Childhood & Elementary School 25

Beliefs & Values. 37

Activity: The Most Important
Thing Dad Taught Me 45

Career & Jobs 57

Activity: Tools of the Trade 67

Love 71

People Who Influenced You 87

Activity: In Your Own Words 93

Education 97

Hobbies & Pastimes 107

Activity: Instagramming Dad 115

Places You Have Lived 119

Activity: Dad Was Here 125

Health & Medical 131

Ancestry & Heritage 137

Activity: Dad's Timeline 147

Travel, Technology & Historic Moments 151

Activity: On This Day in History 159

Completely Random Questions 163

Activity: Googling Dad
& Documenting the Documents 173

Thoughts 175

That Reminds Me 177

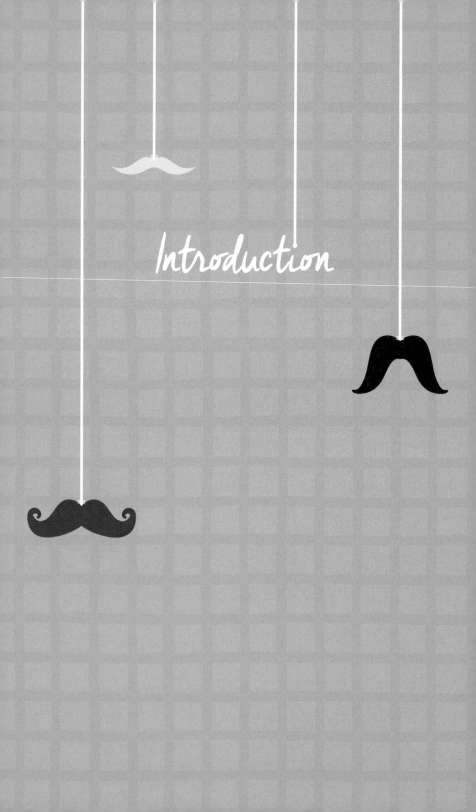

Introduction

Imagine that you know you are going to pass away tomorrow and you have today, and only today, to document your entire life story. You will be allowed to fill a carry-on suitcase with everything you can fit into it that you want to pass on to future generations of your family. This will be the only record they will have of who you were, what you did for a living, who you loved, or what your values were. Your great-grandchildren will only know you based on what you condense into this one small space. What would you put in?

Just for fun, try it. Get a small suitcase and set a timer for twenty minutes. Gather your "most prized possessions" and family heirlooms. Put in your favorite photo albums, the DVD copy of the day you danced with your daughter at her wedding, the silver watch handed down from your grandfather, or your military medals. Dig through your file cabinet and pull out your college diploma and your marriage certificate. Rummage through boxes in the basement or attic until you find your college letterman jacket, the game ball you were given after the state championship, the carved pen set your wife gave you for your first anniversary, the treasured model airplane you and your older brother built together.

What about your baseball card collection you amassed when you were in elementary school, the award you earned as "employee of the year," or the copy of your master's thesis? Once you are finished, stand back and smile. You've gathered all the things you own that are most important to you. But here's the problem. Even this treasury of important items is not likely to have meaning to anyone else because something important is still missing: the stories.

• The gold watch your parents gave you as a graduation gift has long since stopped working. Your kids will throw it away if you don't let them know your dad went without his lunch for six months to save the money to buy it.

• The photo of you at Yellowstone National Park preserves an image of what you looked like, but does it tell the story about how you hitchhiked to get there?

• The ticket stub from a double feature at the Egyptian Theatre is meaningless to anyone who doesn't understand that you saved it because it was the first date you had with your wife.

The memories that are important to you will only be important to the people you love if you share the stories that give them meaning. That is what this book is for. Between the pages of this book, you'll record some of those precious stories and compile, day by day, a history of some of your most important moments.

This will be the only record they will have of who you were, what you did for a living, who you loved, or what your values were.

With over three hundred question prompts, plus pages designed to help you involve your children in the story-gathering process, the memories you record here are destined to become someone else's "most prized possession." Enjoy the journey you are about to take—a journey to record and remember your life's most important moments. Fill out just one page per day, or pick and choose topics that are interesting to you and fill them out in any order. Scribble out the original

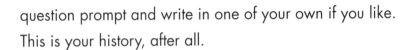

question prompt and write in one of your own if you like. This is your history, after all.

As you write, you'll be reminded of other stories you want to record, and there may or may not be a question prompt in the book that will help you remember that story. To make sure these treasured stories are not forgotten, use the "That Reminds Me" sheets, starting on page 177, to jot down your own story prompts so you can remember to include those stories too.

This book is organized by topic rather than by date, and that's by design. Of course your children will want to know what day you were born and who your parents were. That's why most personal histories start that way. But we prefer to let you dive right in and start telling stories we know your children will love. Rather than being a book that records just names and dates, this book is designed to record stories—your stories.

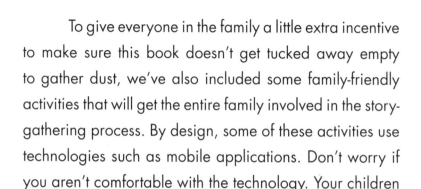

To give everyone in the family a little extra incentive to make sure this book doesn't get tucked away empty to gather dust, we've also included some family-friendly activities that will get the entire family involved in the story-gathering process. By design, some of these activities use technologies such as mobile applications. Don't worry if you aren't comfortable with the technology. Your children probably are. The point is to have some fun family time as you work together to create your living history.

NOTE: If you are giving a copy of this book to your father as a gift, please see the activity, "The Most Important Thing Dad Taught Me" on page 45. You may choose to give members of your family an opportunity to write their own thoughts in this section prior to gifting the book to your dad.

Family Stories

Describe your most memorable family vacation.

What was your most disastrous family vacation? Do you remember a vacation mishap you can laugh about today?

Which sibling were you closest to while growing up? Why?

What is one thing this sibling did for you that you have always been grateful for?

Describe your parents' work. What did your father do for a living? What did your mother do?

_____

_____

_____

_____

_____

_____

What one-on-one experience with your mother stands out in your memory?

_____

_____

_____

_____

_____

_____

_____

_____

_____

_____

_____

_____

What do you remember most about watching your father work around the house or in the yard?

Growing up, what were some family expectations?

Were you named after anyone? What does your name mean?

Do you have a nickname? If so, what is it and who gave it to you?

_____

_____

_____

_____

_____

_____

_____

_____

_____

_____

Did you have a favorite hiding place as a child?

_____

_____

_____

What was your favorite family car?

_____

_____

_____

What do you remember about the day a loved one died? What was the first family funeral you ever attended?

Name each of your children and think of one thing you would specifically leave to them.

_____

_____

_____

_____

_____

_____

_____

_____

_____

_____

_____

What was the favorite children's book your kids asked you to read again and again?

_____

_____

_____

_____

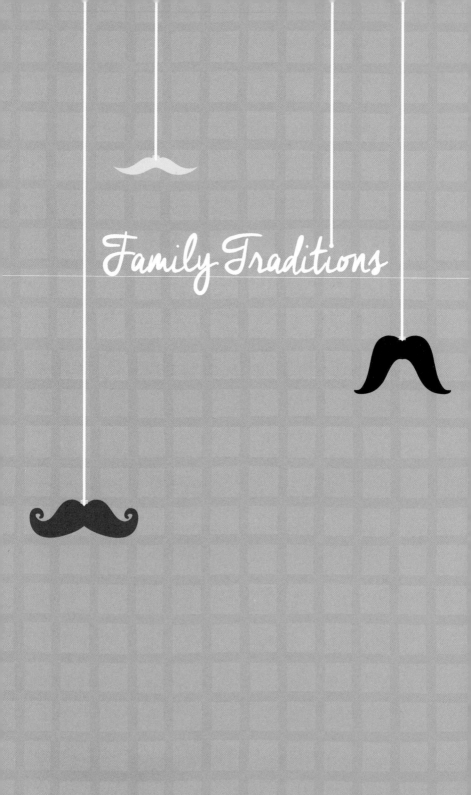

Family Traditions

What are some of your favorite Christmas traditions?

_____

_____

_____

_____

_____

_____

_____

Next to Christmas or Hanukkah, what is your favorite holiday?

_____

_____

_____

_____

How did you most often celebrate the Fourth of July?

_____

_____

Write down any quirky traditions your family keeps when family members have a birthday.

_____

_____

_____

What was your most memorable costume for Halloween?

How much money would the tooth fairy leave under your pillow? What would you buy with it?

What New Year's Eve do you remember the most? Why was it so memorable?

What Thanksgiving tradition did you carry on with your own family?

What is your favorite kind of pie on Thanksgiving?

Describe anything unique your family did to decorate during Halloween, Christmas, or another holiday.

Did you pray together as a family? How did that change your relationship with your parents and siblings?

Did you attend church each week?

Can you recall any other family traditions that were unique to your family?

_____

_____

_____

_____

_____

_____

_____

_____

_____

_____

_____

_____

_____

_____

_____

_____

_____

_____

_____

Activity

The Dad Treasure Hunt

a hunt to help your children discover the whereabouts of
your most prized possessions

Make a treasure map or create a treasure hunt (complete with clues) for your children. Before you start, consider what items are in your home that you would consider treasures, perhaps treasures no one else knows about. You may need to dig through your attic or sock drawer to find things that even you have forgotten about. If you are comfortable with the idea, allow your children to rummage around the house and attic. Have them bring items to you that they find interesting. Consider labeling some of these items to let children know whom you would like to inherit them in the future.

This is not necessarily a treasure hunt to find things that will have value to other people. This is a treasure hunt to document things that are valuable to YOU and the reasons why. Something as simple as a button from one of your uniforms, a wood chess set, or an old pair of your eyeglasses could become a treasure to your children. Once you are gone, even a single tangible item that once belonged to you will give them a connection to you and a story to tell their own children. Remember, all it really takes to turn something into an heirloom is a story and time.

Do you have any of the following items in your home just waiting to become an heirloom?

☐ Paintings, photography, and works of art

☐ Mementos you brought home from vacations or business trips

☐ Photographs and photo albums

☐ Family Bible

☐ Jewelry and other personal items that are important to you, regardless of their "cash value"

☐ A photo of the first car you owned

☐ Medals and trophies

☐ A coat, uniform, or article of clothing you have saved

☐ Valuable books (early, first edition copies, signed copies, or just your favorites)

- [ ] A gift you received for your wedding

- [ ] An item given to you by a special friend or acquaintance

- [ ] Old slides, DVDs, VHS tapes, cassette tapes, or computer disks you have saved because of their historical significance

- [ ] Glasses, watches, or things that stopped working, but you kept anyway

- [ ] A gift your wife gave you while you were courting or as an anniversary present

- [ ] Anything handed down to you by your own parents or grandparents

- [ ] "Vintage" toys or games you have saved

- [ ] Favorite music or albums

Childhood & Elementary School

Where were you born?

What was unique about your birth?

What is your earliest memory?

What was the name of the elementary school you attended?

Who was your favorite elementary school teacher? What was especially memorable about that teacher? What did you appreciate most about him/her?

Did you earn any awards or recognitions when you were in elementary school (prior to age twelve)?

_____

_____

_____

How did you prefer to spend your time at recess?

_____

_____

_____

Is there a memorable school or church performance you participated in as a child?

_____

_____

_____

Who was your best friend in elementary school? What do you remember doing together that was so fun?

_____

_____

_____

What was a common after-school activity you participated in?

_____

_____

How long did it take you to get to and from school? How did you get there? Do you have a memorable experience related to getting back and forth from school?

_____

_____

_____

_____

_____

_____

_____

What stands out in your memory about the school, playground, or principal? Was there anything unusual about the school?

_____

_____

_____

_____

_____

_____

_____

_____

Describe your school lunch. What was in it? Who made it?

How did you celebrate Halloween, Valentine's Day, or other holidays at school?

Did you have any pets? What were their names? Describe a happy or sad event with one of them.

_____

_____

_____

_____

_____

_____

_____

What did you want to be when you grew up?

_____

_____

Did you play a musical instrument as a child?

_____

_____

What is the worst thing you ever did that you never got in trouble for because no one but you knew about it?

_____

_____

_____

_____

What is something you hesitated telling your parents about for fear of being punished? Did you confess later?

_____

_____

_____

_____

_____

_____

What was your favorite thing to wear as a child?

_____

_____

Do you have a birthday that stands out as particularly memorable? Why?

_____

_____

_____

_____

_____

Describe a time when you went with a parent to buy groceries.

How much did a postage stamp cost when you were a child?

Who cut your hair when you were growing up? What was your most embarrassing hairstyle as a child?

Describe a typical day at kindergarten.

What did you do during school holidays?

What was your best subject in school? What was your worst subject?

Did you ever visit the principal's office?

Describe the meanest teacher you ever had in school, or the class you least preferred to attend.

What kind of antics would go on when you had a substitute in the classroom? Describe an example.

Describe a trip to the library when you were a child. Did you have your own library card? What kinds of books did you like to read?

Describe a trip downtown or to the "big city" that you took as a youngster.

What was your greatest fear as a child? Why do you think you were so afraid of this?

How old were you when you learned to ride a bike? Who taught you?

Who taught you to swim, and where did you learn?

Describe an adventure you had as a child.

Did you have a favorite movie?

Who was your "first love" or childhood crush?

Did you have your own room? If not, who did you share a room with?

What was your favorite room in your house growing up?

_____

Did you live in more than one house as a child? How many times did you move before you were eighteen, and why?

_____
_____
_____
_____
_____

Did you play sports growing up? If so, which ones?

_____
_____
_____

Who was your favorite movie star, singer, or athlete?

_____
_____

What was a common saying or "slang" term you and your friends used when you were growing up?

_____
_____

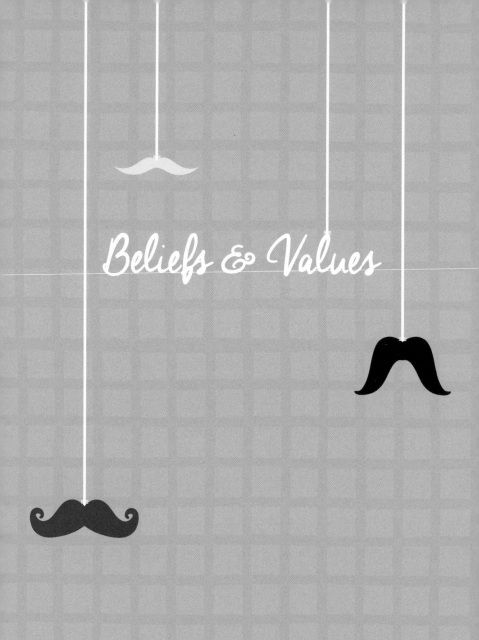

Beliefs & Values

Do you belong to a particular church, religious, or civic organization?

What is your earliest memory of attending church with your family? If you never attended a church, what is your earliest memory of someone you respected teaching you an important value, principle, or belief?

Do you consider yourself to be a person of faith? Why or why not?

Describe a time you remember being untruthful. What were the circumstances and how did you feel about the experience afterward?

_____
_____
_____
_____
_____
_____
_____

Describe an average Saturday or Sunday from your childhood.

_____
_____
_____
_____
_____
_____
_____
_____
_____
_____

Have you ever had a very difficult time forgiving someone for something? What happened?

What are your thoughts about prayer? Have you ever had a prayer answered in a miraculous way?

Describe any work you have done to provide humanitarian service to someone less fortunate than you.

Describe a time when you experienced a terrible loss. How did you begin to heal from or overcome the loss?

Have you ever done something dishonest you regretted? How did you make amends? What advice would you give your children or grandchildren to help them avoid making the same mistake?

_____

_____

_____

Did you have a favorite Bible or scripture story? If so, what was it?

_____

_____

_____

Is there a family story that was told over and over again that taught you a particular value, such as "why it's important to tell the truth," "why you should never give up," or "why you should never criticize another person"?

_____

_____

_____

_____

Did you serve in your church? What was your favorite way to serve?

_____

_____

What do you firmly believe in?

What advice would you give your children about faith?

What were some of your favorite religious or spiritual activities and traditions?

Did you have your own scriptures? If so, when were they given to you? By whom?

What is one spiritual experience that changed the course of your life?

_____
_____
_____
_____

If you could go back and understand one truth earlier, what would that be?

_____
_____
_____

When was the first time you remember feeling the Spirit?

_____
_____
_____

What prayer was not answered how you wanted it to be, but it turned out for the best?

_____
_____
_____
_____

Activity

The Most Important Thing Dad Taught Me

thoughts and memories from your children

This section is reserved for your children to write in. Give each of them an opportunity to write their thoughts about the most important thing they have learned from you. Alternately, they may prefer to write their best memory of you. Several blank pages have also been provided for children who prefer to draw their happiest memories. Don't forget to have your children date and sign the page.

Career & Jobs

What was your first job and what wage did you earn? Describe the working conditions and anything unusual about your job.

What did you do with the cash you earned from your earliest jobs?

What is something you bought or paid for with your own money that you were excited about?

Describe any chores you were expected to do around your home growing up.

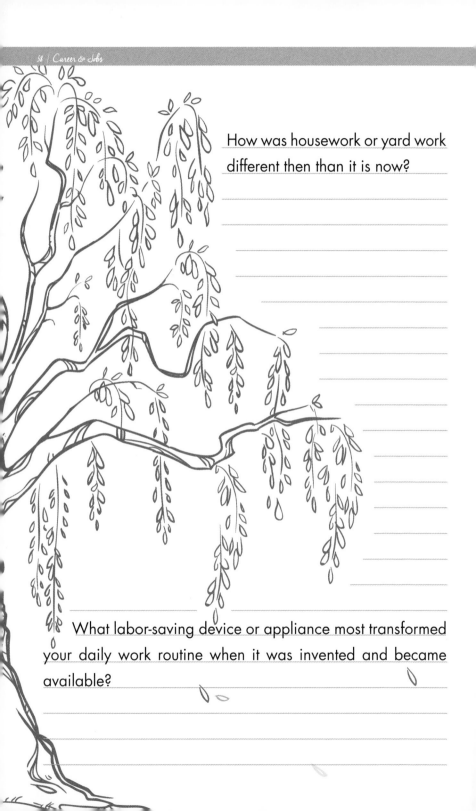

How was housework or yard work different then than it is now?

_____
_____
_____
_____
_____
_____
_____
_____
_____
_____
_____
_____

What labor-saving device or appliance most transformed your daily work routine when it was invented and became available?

_____
_____
_____

What was the most unique job you ever had?

_____

_____

_____

Did you ever start any kind of entrepreneurial adventure?

_____

_____

_____

Did you or anyone in your family serve in the military? If so, what do you want your children to know about the experience?

_____

_____

_____

_____

_____

Describe a typical day at work in your chosen career. What duties did you enjoy the most?

_____

_____

_____

Describe your most annoying coworker and tell what made this peson so difficult to work with.

_____

_____

_____

_____

Was there a boss or supervisor who taught you something significant or important that you used for the rest of your career?

_____

_____

_____

How do you feel your career allowed you to make a difference in the world?

_____

_____

_____

_____

Did you ever go on a memorable business trip or attend a conference that impacted your career in a significant way?

_____

_____

_____

Would you recommend your career to your children? Why or why not?

_____

_____

_____

_____

_____

_____

_____

_____

If you had your whole life to do over again, is there another career you think you would have liked to pursue?

_____

_____

_____

Were there any barriers to employment you had to overcome?

_____

_____

_____

_____

What is the most significant contribution you ever made to your employer in terms of an idea, process, or habit that helped make the company more profitable or successful?

Were you ever fired from a job? Can you tell about the experience and what you learned from it?

What job did you love the most?

What job did you have that you worked the hardest at and made the least amount of money?

How did you choose your occupation?

When did you decide you had landed your "dream" job?

_____
_____
_____
_____
_____

If you could have your children experience one of the jobs or chores you used to do consistently that they will never have to do, what would it be? What would you hope for them to learn from it?

_____
_____
_____
_____
_____
_____
_____
_____
_____
_____
_____
_____
_____

What career accomplishment are you proudest of?

Did your parents want you to choose the profession you did?

What time did you go to and get home from work each day?

Activity
Tools of the Trade

Regardless of your career or your favorite hobbies, it's likely that you acquired a set of special "tools" to perform your work. If you were an artist, you may have had a favorite set of brushes or a particular brand of canvas you preferred. An accountant's tools might include a ten-key adding machine or a particular software package. Whether your tool of choice was a wrench or a whistle, a walkie-talkie or a T square, you very likely have tools in your desk, workshop, toolbox, or shed that have been with you for years—a brand of pen you always used, a hammer whose shaft fit your hand perfectly, a Rolodex of business cards you couldn't do without.

The purpose of this activity is to gather your five most "valuable" tools and document how and where you used them. It's likely that your own children have never been able to watch you work for any extended period of time. Since your career made up such an important part of your life, this is just one way of showing them how you made your mark in the world. What were the tools of your trade?

If you aren't able to access the actual implement you used to use, a photo from the Internet is fine. This "show and tell" activity will give your children an opportunity to learn something about you and your method of work they would have no other way of knowing about. Do they know what a slide rule looks like? Have they ever watched you use your stethoscope or your handgun? If you have any tools that were passed down to you by your own father or grandfather, be sure to show these off as well.

Once you've gathered your "Tools of the Trade," consider any other fun, age-appropriate options you might have for helping your children understand your work. This could include anything from taking a child for a ride in your squad car to arranging a tour of the facility where you work. It could mean setting up a "pretend" office for an afternoon and letting your kids play with an old, used computer keyboard or cell phone. A single opportunity to view your workplace—spin in your office chair, smell the grease in the pit where you do oil changes, or write on the whiteboard in the conference room—will create lasting memories for your children and give them a more complete picture of who you are and how you made your living.

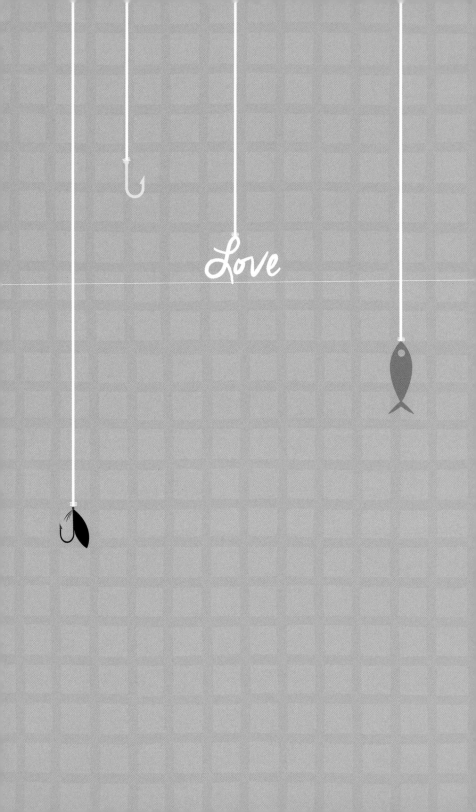

Describe your first date ever. Where did you go, and what did you do together?

What was the most unusual or creative date you ever went on?

Did you ever ask someone on a date or answer an invitation to a date in a unique way?

Describe what happened and how you felt the first time you broke up with a girlfriend.

Describe the outfit your spouse was wearing the first time you met, or any other details you remember about the first time you saw your spouse.

_____

_____

_____

_____

_____

Describe, in some detail, the process you typically used when you asked a girl on a date. How was dating different then than it is now?

_____

_____

_____

_____

_____

_____

Describe your first date with your spouse. What was your first impression after this date? What was the one thing you noticed about her that intrigued you most?

Describe two characteristics you most admire in your spouse.

What do you remember about your first kiss? What about the first time you kissed your wife?

_____

_____

_____

_____

_____

_____

_____

_____

_____

_____

Describe some details about how your romance progressed. What are some fun experiences you had while courting?

_____

_____

When did you first know you were in love?

How did you propose? What is the one emotion from that day that stands out above all of the others?

Did you ever buy your wife an expensive piece of jewelry other than her wedding ring?

Where were you married? Give a few memorable details from your wedding day. (If you have been married more than once, feel free to share details about each wedding.)

Where did you go on your honeymoon? Are there any humorous or interesting stories you like to tell others about your honeymoon?

What is the most romantic thing your spouse ever did for you?
Give details.

What would you consider to be the most romantic thing you've
ever done for your spouse?

Did your wife call you by any pet names? Did those names
change over the years?

Do you treat your spouse better, worse, or about the same as you did while you were dating or courting?

_____

_____

_____

What is the most important thing you have learned about being married?

_____

_____

_____

_____

_____

What advice would you give your children about choosing a companion?

_____

_____

_____

What was your favorite date activity while you were dating?

What is the worst date you ever went on?

What dance in high school was your most memorable?

Did you ever feel guilty accepting a date? Why?

What are the qualities you were looking for in a spouse? Are those the same qualities that you would look for today?

_____

_____

_____

_____

_____

What was the make and model of the car (or other method of transportation) you typically used during your courting years?

_____

_____

_____

Describe meeting your wife's parents for the first time. What was your first impression of them?

_____

_____

_____

_____

What did your parents think of your spouse?

_____

_____

_____

Did you feel a spiritual connection with your spouse?

How did you know your spouse was the right one?

When were you the angriest at your spouse?

Do you have a favorite love note from your spouse? What did it say? If you have it, attach it here.

If appropriate, write a paragraph or two about the most important thing you learned after being married.

People Who
Influenced You

What is the best advice anyone ever gave you? What was accomplished by following that advice?

Who was your best friend in high school? What stands out in your mind as a time when you really leaned on and appreciated this friend?

Who is your "oldest" friend?

Name two of your most influential high school teachers and what they taught you.

If you attended college, what professor influenced you the most? Why?

Is there a coworker, business partner, boss, or supervisor you feel you owe a debt of gratitude to? Why?

Is there someone you once hated who you later developed a more respectful relationship with? What changed?

Who taught you about faith?

What do you remember most
about your father's influence?

_____
_____
_____
_____
_____
_____
_____
_____
_____
_____
_____

Were you closer to one grandfather than another?
If so, why do you think that was?

_____
_____
_____
_____

What do you remember most about your mother's influence?

Who was your favorite example or role model growing up?

What is the quality you value most in a friend?

Which sibling would you want to be compared to?

Activity

In Your Own Words

recording your voice

One of the treasured memories you can preserve for your family, using a host of new technologies, is a simple audio or video recording. With mobile device technology, there's almost no excuse not to have recordings of several special moments.

Treasured memories can be preserved using a simple audio or video recording.

One of the largest family history-related sites on the Internet is FamilySearch.org. FamilySearch has created a "Memories" app that allows users to quickly record photos and voice memos and upload these "Memories" to the FamilySearch website. Stories archived on the site will be accessible for generations to come. The fun thing about this resource is that it will allow you to record multiple stories about your life, in your own voice. Visit the app website for details: https://familysearch.org /mobile/memories. With the app, you simply record yourself telling a story about your personal history using a smartphone or mobile device. Once the recording is completed and saved, you can instantly upload the recording to the FamilySearch website. (You can also "tag" the names of other family members mentioned in the story.) Once you "attach" a story to a specific individual's FamilySearch profile, people outside of your immediate family will not be able to see or access these recordings until after the individual is deceased. This helps maintain privacy for living persons.

Note to children: Take the time to sit Dad down and record at least three or four of his favorite personal stories. Generations of future grandchildren and great-grandchildren will thank you some day. It will give them the ability to hear his voice and learn about his personality in ways that written documents can't capture.

Use some of the questions from this book as inspiration, or, if you want to create a video instead, set your mobile device on a stable surface, and capture Dad's legacy by creating a permanent record for others to enjoy. He'll probably be uneasy the first time you try it. People are often uncomfortable hearing their own recorded voice or watching a video of themselves, so you may need to try a couple of times to get your dad to warm up to the idea.

If you decide to upload your recordings online, or to FamilySearch, keep these important points in mind:

1. Make sure you add a detailed title to your recording so others will know what it is about and will be enticed to listen.

2. Because most of us have a pretty short attention span, it's usually best to record short two to three minute segments and upload several of them than it is to upload a single long recording that includes several stories.

Education

Was there ever a "first day of school" that was particularly difficult for you?

Describe your most memorable day in junior high or high school.

Think of a time when a teacher said or did something that hurt your feelings.

Do you have a memorized poem or section of prose you like to recite during difficult or important times in your life?

_____

_____

_____

_____

_____

_____

Did your education ever get cut short? If so, why?

_____

_____

_____

_____

_____

_____

_____

What dream or goal did you have as a teenager that you accomplished? That you didn't accomplish?

_____

_____

_____

_____

_____

Think of a time when you got into the most trouble with a teacher. What did they do to handle the problem?

What was your high school mascot? What were your school colors? Did these influence the way you dressed at school, and if so, how?

Describe a typical high school date. Where did kids your age like to hang out and what did you like to do on dates?

Did you ever attend a prom or formal dance? Describe the experience.

Describe any clubs or student organizations you were involved in.

Can you remember a tragedy or other significant world event that happened when you were in high school? Did this affect your personal future at all?

What award or accomplishment from your high school days stands out as the most significant?

How many students were in your high school graduating class?

What did you do for your graduation celebration?

After high school, what was the next step in your life plan—work, college, vocational school, military, or humanitarian experience? Give some details about why you made that decision and why you are glad you took that path.

If you attended a college or vocational school, tell about what you studied, what you majored or minored in. If you completed a master's degree or PhD, describe your thesis and dissertation.

What is the most important thing your children could do after they graduate from high school that will help prepare them for life?

Tell about any roommates you had, including quirky habits they had.

During your early twenties, what kind of recreational pursuits did you enjoy as a break from the routine of work or school?

Did you like to learn?

What was the one thing you wish you would have paid more attention to in school?

Did you drive a car to school? What kind?

What was your favorite subject?

Were you ever teased or bullied?

Did you receive a scholarship or grant?

Did you ever feel like giving up? Name one experience when you were not sure school was for you.

Did your parents encourage education? Did they expect you to attend college?

Was there a class or teacher that helped you decide what career path to take? How did the class or teacher spark your interest?

Hobbies & Pastimes

What sports did you play as a child?

_____

_____

_____

Did you ever have your photo in a newspaper?

_____

_____

_____

_____

Have you ever entered a project or an item into a fair, contest, or competition? Why did you win or lose?

_____

_____

_____

As a child, did you take any kind of lessons? If so, describe the teacher and what you learned.

_____

_____

_____

Did you ever have an experience with losing a contest or hearing someone criticize something you were really proud of? What was your reaction?

_____

_____

_____

What is one talent you started to develop but gave up? Why did you stop?

What is one talent you think you could have really excelled in if time, desire, or money had been more plentiful?

Have you ever performed in public? If so, what was your most memorable performance ever?

Have you ever participated on a team? Think of two or three examples and tell what was memorable about it.

Describe a teammate you admired or despised and explain why you felt the way you did.

What act of selfless service did you perform at one time in your life that required more of you than you expected it to? Describe what happened.

Was there ever a pet in your home you had a special relationship with?

Do you have any memorable experiences hunting, fishing, or working with animals in the wild?

Recall a visit to a theme park or fair that did or didn't turn out like you expected.

Describe the worst campout you ever went on.

Concert, rodeo, or baseball game—which would you choose and why?

_____
_____
_____
_____

Did you ever take swimming lessons?

_____
_____
_____
_____

Describe one of your hobbies and how you developed an interest in that hobby.

_____
_____
_____
_____
_____

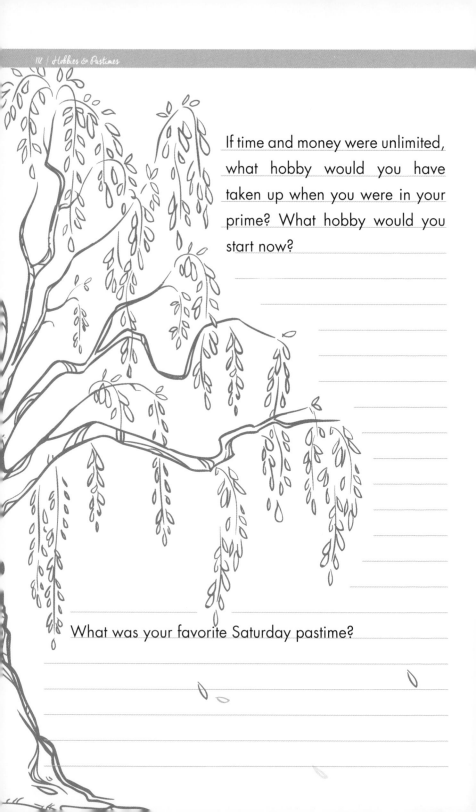

If time and money were unlimited, what hobby would you have taken up when you were in your prime? What hobby would you start now?

_____

_____

_____

_____

_____

_____

_____

_____

_____

_____

What was your favorite Saturday pastime?

_____

_____

_____

_____

What age were you when you first saw the ocean?

_____

_____

_____

_____

If you could choose, in hindsight, one thing you wish you had participated in during high school, what would it be?

_____

_____

_____

_____

_____

_____

Who was your favorite coach?

_____

_____

_____

_____

_____

_____

Activity

Instagramming Dad

Here's a fun activity that any child with a mobile device can help you complete. Have your son or daughter photograph you in ten different settings of their choosing and post the favorite one to Instagram using the hashtag, **#InstagrammingDad**. If you search for #InstagrammingDad, you'll find fun photos other *Dad's Storybook* readers have taken with their fathers, and you may just find some inspiration.

Start with some of these ideas:

☐ Dad in his workshop, at his desk, or in a location you would commonly find him

☐ Him with something that is related to one of his hobbies (a set of season football tickets, a computer, woodworking tools, a fishing pole)

☐ His oldest, most "vintage" household gadget or tool

☐ His bedroom or office

☐ Everything he keeps in the glove compartment in his car, or everything he keeps on the nightstand next to his bed

☐ His hands

☐ Dad holding "his most priceless possession"

☐ Something that represents your favorite recreational pastime with Dad—Dad astride his four-wheeler, behind the steering wheel of his boat, or with his golf clubs

☐ Dad with something he made or built

☐ A truly "candid" photo of Dad with Mom

As an alternative, sit down with your child to create a time capsule of the twenty most important photos of you that exist. What photos would your child choose? What photos would you choose?

Consider the following:

- How will the family preserve these important photos?

- Who will be responsible to keep and care for the originals?

- How can copies of the originals be made available to anyone who is interested? (See page 93 for information about using the FamilySearch Memories app to preserve a copy online for extended family and future generations to access.)

- Are there other photos in your collection that include pictures of people only you can identify?

- What is the best way to document and archive your most precious family photos?

Places You Have Lived

What was the community of your childhood like? What did your neighborhood look like?

Can you remember any details about the home you grew up in (or your favorite place you lived if you moved around a lot)?

Describe the first apartment or house you lived in when you moved away from your parents' home for the first time.

Would you prefer to live in the city or the country if you were twenty-one and just starting out? Why?

Think of a neighbor who had an impact on you. Was he or she friendly or grouchy? Why does the memory of that person stand out to you?

What did you do during the summer with friends who lived in your neighborhood?

Did you ever have a get-together or block party with your neighbors?

Describe your neighborhood as an adult. What neighbors do you remember best and why?

How many times did you move growing up?

If you could choose any place to live now, where would that be?

Did you ever hate living somewhere? What about it did you hate?

What is the longest you ever lived somewhere?

How close was your church or place of worship?

Activity

Dad Was Here

If you've ever carved your name in a tree trunk, put your initials in wet cement, or even defaced the door of a bathroom stall, you will have some sense that many of us like to document our existence with something "permanent." And what is more permanent than the home you live in? Much of your life has been spent providing "the comforts of home" for your family, so why not preserve a few photos and stories of your home, or any other geographic location that bears the stamp of your handiwork? In just one afternoon, you can document some photos and details about the home you live in, and if you've lived in lots of places, there's a way to document that as well.

Begin by taking a photograph of each of the rooms of your existing home. These don't need to be staged. Your children will have fond memories of the piles of paper on the floor in your office or the sawdust piles in your shop. What will bring back fond memories for them is the way your home looked when you lived there. Once you are gone, these photos will bring back happy memories of eating pretzels on the couch with you during a football game, or helping you clean leaves out of the rain gutters every fall.

After you have photographed the exterior of your home, and a few of the larger rooms, take a few close-ups of specific items that will have significance or hold memories for you and for others. See http://www.agenerousthought.com/The-House-That-Bart-Built/ for a sample of some of the kinds of stories a house can tell.

Watch for opportunities to photograph some of the following items:

- Military history—Any mementos, photos, or uniforms you still have

- Your favorite brand of aftershave

- Your car, truck, motorcycle, or other favorite mode of transportation

- A photo of your favorite brand of candy

- Pictures of things you might commonly find in your pockets

- A photo of what the lunchbox you carried to work looked like

- A photo of your work uniform, overalls, work boots, and so on

- A musical instrument you play

  - Your bookshelf, or a few of the books you consider to be life-changing

  If there's a special spot where the kids like to hide, or a closet where you keep the toys they play with most often, make sure to document these with a photo as well. You can even turn the photos into a fun photo book using a book creation website like www.blurb.com, www.shutterfly.com, www.lulu.com, justfamily.com, or even a book creation tool from your local photofinishing establishment. Online apps like chatbook.com can download right from your Instagram feed and mail you a finished book at an economical price.

Here are a couple of ideas for making the book fun:

☐ Create a "Dad's ABC Book" by taking photographs of items in your home that start with each letter of the alphabet. Include a sentence or two of explanatory information such as, "H is for Helicopter. Dad flew a V-22 Osprey Tiltrotor during the War in Iraq and built this model helicopter himself."

☐ Hide an item such as a one of your child's favorite stuffed animals in plain sight in each room before you take a photograph. Once this "Hide and Seek at Home" book is finished, your child can hunt for the hidden item in each picture.

☐ Using the same idea, title your book, "Dad's I Spy Book" and give your child a list of things to find in each room: "Find the world globe, the picture of Mom, an upside-down pillow, two lamps, and a marble camouflaged on the oriental rug."

If you've relocated homes often, and your children don't necessarily associate you with a particular home or apartment, you can create your book by documenting some of the other places you have lived or traveled. Use a combination of stock photographs of buildings you love, places where you studied, or buildings where you worked.

Health & Medical

Did you ever have a disease that children are now vaccinated against? Mumps? Polio? Measles? Chicken pox? Describe what it was like.

What was the strangest medicine you ever had to take as a child? Why did you need to take it?

Describe what it was like to be sick when you were a child.

Were there any home remedies used in your family to cure illness or injury? Can you describe in detail how they worked?

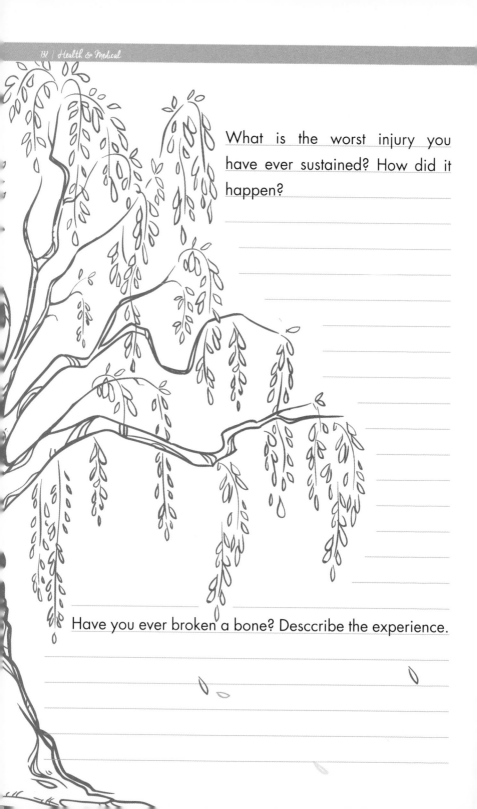

What is the worst injury you
have ever sustained? How did it
happen?

Have you ever broken a bone? Desccribe the experience.

Do you have any interesting memories related to the births of any of your children?

Talk about your most memorable trip to the dentist, or what you remember a visit to the dentist being like when you were young.

Did you ever see an orthodontist? What strange and unique orthodontic devices did you wear as a child or as an adult?

Were you afraid of the dentist?

Did you ever have a faith-building experience that had to do with your health?

If you could change one part of your medical history, what would it be?

If you could have had one medical miracle, what would it be?

Were you ever in a car accident?

Were you ever injured on the job or while playing sports? How did this injury impact you?

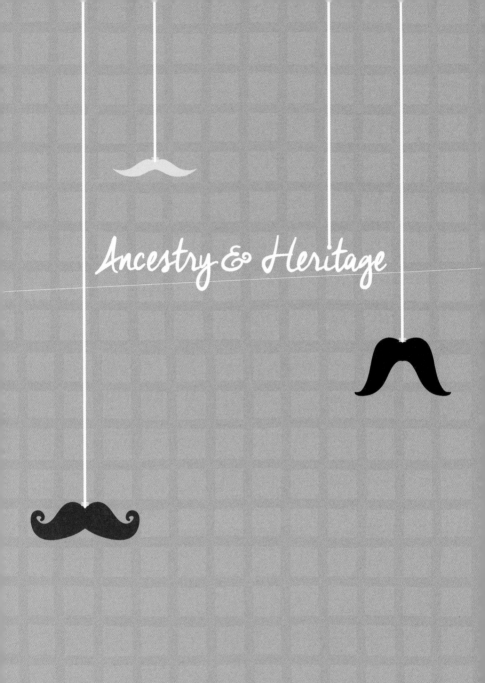

Ancestry & Heritage

What's your mother's name and birthplace?

What's your father's name and birthplace?

If your mother or father has passed away, what do you recall about their death? How old were you at the time?

What do you want your children to know about your mother?

What characteristic do you most admire about your mother?

What was your favorite thing to do with your mother?

What do you want your children to know about your father?

_____

_____

_____

_____

_____

_____

_____

What characteristic do you most admire about your father?

_____

_____

_____

_____

_____

What was your favorite thing to do with your father?

_____

_____

_____

_____

_____

_____

What is the one story your mother told over and over about herself?

What was your parents' most common form of discipline when you were disobedient? Do you agree or disagree with their methods?

What hobby or talent was your dad known for?

What hobby or talent was your mom known for?

What is one story you heard your father tell about himself more than once?

_____

_____

_____

_____

_____

_____

_____

_____

_____

What is a phrase you heard your mother say often?

_____

_____

What is a phrase you heard your father say often?

_____

_____

_____

Tell something you remember about watching your dad get ready for work.

_____

_____

Whenever you smell _____, it reminds you of your mom. Why?

_____

_____

_____

_____

What parenting advice did your parents or others give you that you implemented in your own home with some success?

_____

_____

_____

_____

_____

_____

Who was your favorite aunt or uncle? Why?

_____

_____

_____

_____

What was your favorite thing to do with your grandpa?

Did you live near any extended family growing up?

What phrase did you hate hearing your mom say?

How did you know when your dad was proud of you?

Did you ever have an experience where you felt really close to your mother?

_____

_____

_____

_____

_____

_____

_____

_____

_____

_____

_____

_____

What car did your grandparents drive?

_____

_____

What do you wish your father would have told you?

What is the best advice your grandma gave you?

Activity

Dad's Timeline

On the following page, you'll find a hundred-year timeline you and your children can use to create a timeline of your major life events. Start by writing in the year of your birth in the first slot on the left, and then write in each succeeding decade.

Next, draw diagonal or horizontal lines that correspond to significant dates in your life. Write the full date on the line you draw and give a brief explanation underneath the date.

Here are examples of dates to record:

1966: I was born in Seattle, Washington.

1988: I graduated from college with a degree in chemical engineering.

1990: I married my high school sweetheart, Madge.

2001: The day our first son was born. His name is Brian.

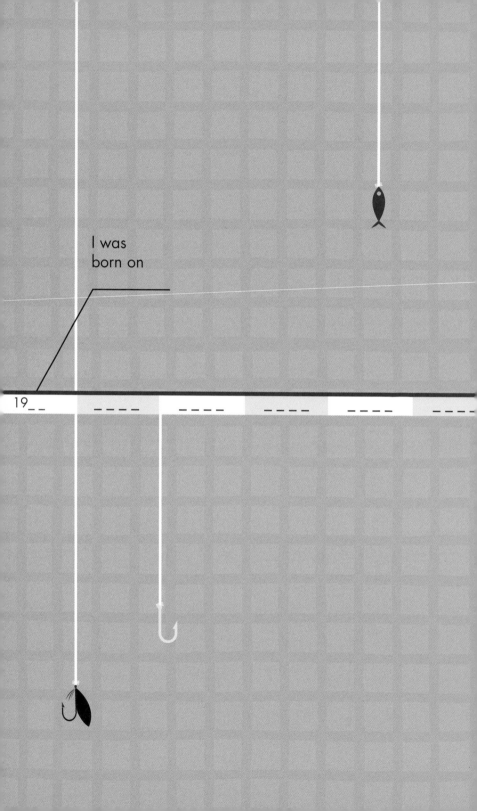

I was
born on

19_ _

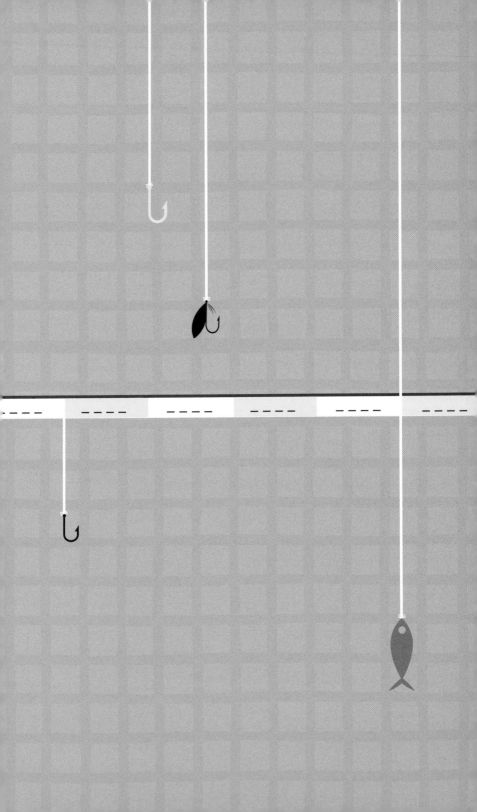

Travel, Technology & Historic Moments

What is your dream car?

Describe your first car. What did you like about it? How much did it cost? What was unique about it?

Think of three unusual forms of transportation you have used. What were the circumstances?

Did you ever get a flat tire or have car problems when it was particularly inconvenient?

Name a time when you were stranded. What happened?
How did you get yourself out of the situation?

When was the first time you remember using a computer?

What was your experience like the first time you sent an email?

Describe your first computer. What were you amazed that it
could do?

Describe your first cell phone and everything you used it for. What did it look like? What was something amazing that you could do with it that no one would be impressed with now? What was the most frustrating thing about it?

Name something that has been invented in your lifetime that you now use every day, other than a computer or cell phone.

When you hear the word, "drive-in," what picture comes to your mind? Describe it.

Describe a time you were pulled over for a traffic violation.

_____

_____

_____

Tell about a time when you traveled to a foreign country. If you
have never traveled, where would you go given the chance?

_____

_____

_____

_____

_____

_____

_____

_____

_____

What is the largest meeting (not a sporting event) you ever
attended? Where was the meeting and what was the purpose?

_____

_____

_____

What would you consider to be the most significant world event that has taken place in your lifetime?

Who taught you how to drive? Describe your earliest memories of what it was like to be behind the wheel, including what you drove and any accidents you had.

What cartoon or TV program did you love as a child?

Describe the first video game you ever played. What was your favorite video or computer game and why?

Describe the first day a man landed on the moon. Where were you and what do you remember about the day?

Describe the first time you remember watching a color TV.

What was the first movie you remember watching? Describe the theater, the movie, and anything else that is different from watching movies now. How has this technology changed during your lifetime?

Describe what you remember about any of the following:
The fall of the Twin Towers on 9/11

The fall of the Berlin Wall

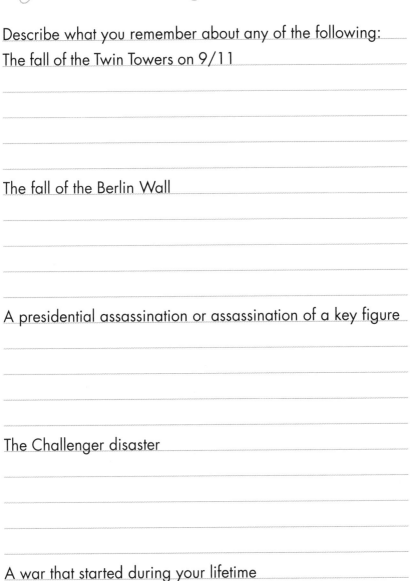

A presidential assassination or assassination of a key figure

The Challenger disaster

A war that started during your lifetime

Activity

On This Day in History

Did you know that January 11 is National "Step in a Puddle and Splash Your Friend Day" or that September 14 is National Cream-filled Donut Day? Do you remember that the Beatles' "We Can Work It Out" was one of the top songs for 1966 and that the price of gas averaged about thirty-two cents per gallon? If you are having difficulty filling out your timeline because your memory is a little rusty, you may be able to search for some of the answers for important historical facts about your lifetime via the Internet. To get you started, see if you can find answers for the following questions:

What crazy national holiday falls on your birthday? Visit https://www.daysoftheyear.com/

What was the weather like on your wedding day? Search http://www.almanac.com/calendar/birthday/09/29

What significant national or international news event occurred the same day you turned forty? Visit the History channel's "This Day in History" http://www.history.com /this-day-in-history page to find out. (Click the "view calendar" link to select different dates).

_____

_____

_____

What was the price of gasoline, the most popular TV show, and the song that was at the top of the billboard charts the day you graduated from high school? Visit http://dmarie.com/timecap/step1.asp to access a "quick page" with the answers.

_____

_____

_____

_____

What box office hits were playing the year you first met your wife? Search http://www.the-numbers.com/movies /index.php#YearIndex

_____

_____

Completely Random
Questions

What is the biggest hole you have ever dug and why?

Did you ever have a brush with the law?

Were you ever lost in a remote place?

Do you have a favorite meal? Is this different or the same as when you were a child?

Think of a time when you were most afraid? Why? What happened?

Was there a storm you experienced that was unusual or memorable? What happened? Were you prepared, afraid, or in awe?

Think of two or three songs, popular, country, or classical, that are your favorites. Why are they important to you and who are the artists?

If it were a blue sky day and you had no other obligations, what would you do with your time? Write down the details of another blue sky day that stands out as a memorable or happy day.

When was a time you were totally alone?

_____

_____

_____

_____

_____

_____

What is the closest you have ever come to experiencing a natural disaster? If you survived one or more disasters, share the details and how experiencing that event affected you personally.

_____

_____

_____

_____

_____

_____

_____

_____

_____

What was a fashion trend you got really excited about?

Describe a birthday party you had as an adult. What stood out about it? Who was present and how did you celebrate?

What is a compliment someone gave you once that you still remember? Who gave you the compliment and why was it so meaningful?

What is your favorite dessert? Describe a time when you recall eating this dessert.

What music, hymn, or song would you like to have performed at your funeral? Why?

_____

_____

_____

_____

_____

_____

Have you ever witnessed something you consider to be a miracle?

_____

_____

_____

_____

_____

_____

_____

_____

What is the dirtiest you have ever been?

What is the hungriest you have ever been?

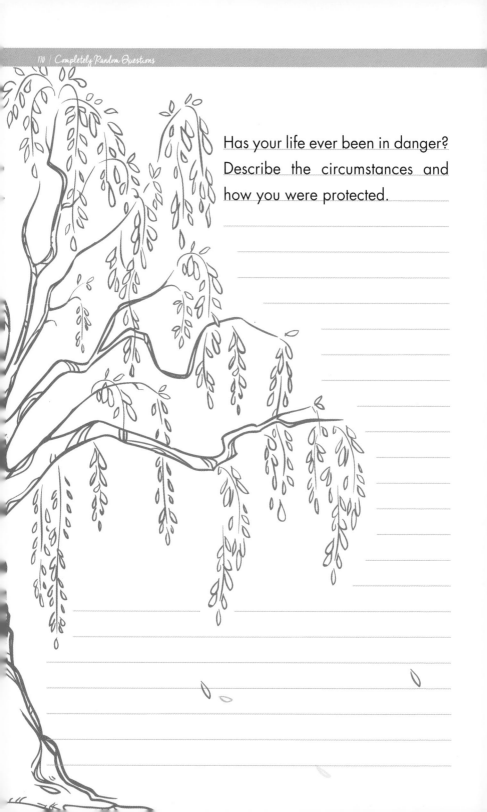

Has your life ever been in danger?
Describe the circumstances and
how you were protected.

Have you ever had to hide from someone or something? Describe the experience.

What was the most embarrassing thing that ever happened to you?

Activity

Googling Dad &
Documenting the Documents

Sit at a computer with one of your children. Have your child show you what he or she can learn about you using only your name as an Internet search term (put quotation marks around your name for a more exact search). You may be shocked how many or how few facts the two of you can document. Try different versions of your name (with and without initials) to get different results. Keep in mind that if you don't leave other records with your family members, this is all your great-grandchildren will know about you. Is the record complete enough to satisfy you or them?

Your life history can be sparsely pieced together just from a few simple documents. Consider how much you would know about a person if all you had access to was an obituary. Family history buffs get excited about details as simple as a birth date or the name of a spouse, because having one piece of accurate information often makes it possible to trace other pieces. You can make the family genealogist's job much easier by compiling originals or copies of a few simple documents. It's easy to store these in a large three-ring binder, using acid-free plastic sheet protectors. The list of documents below pertains specifically to items that will tell part of your "story."

While you are collecting documents to keep together in one safe place, consider adding important papers such as insurance policies or a copy of your will or trust. Speak with a financial planner for a complete list of documents your heirs will need in order to settle your estate.

- ☐ Your birth certificate
- ☐ Your marriage certificate
- ☐ Your written journals or day planner records
- ☐ Photo albums, scrapbooks, or a typewritten page documenting their existence and location
- ☐ Any important letters or correspondence you have saved
- ☐ Your passport or other travel documents
- ☐ Your diploma or degree certificates
- ☐ Your military records and awards
- ☐ A copy of your business card or stationery
- ☐ School awards, trophies, or certificates
- ☐ Medical/health records

Thoughts

If you've written even a single page in this book, congratulations! You've just turned your edition of *Dad's Storybook* into a family heirloom. You've also created a record of your own life, in your own words, and by your own hand, so that your children's children's children will be able to access their own family narrative. That connection to you will be an important part of what they need to get them through rough days and give them a renewed appreciation for their own opportunities and blessings. Looking into the palms of their own hands, they will see you there. They will know you and love you. Even better, they will know you love them.

That Reminds Me

Often, as you begin writing your story, you'll recall a special event, story, or thought you know should be recorded, and you won't want to leave those stories out! Use the following pages to jot down any stories you don't want to "slip through the cracks" and be forgotten.

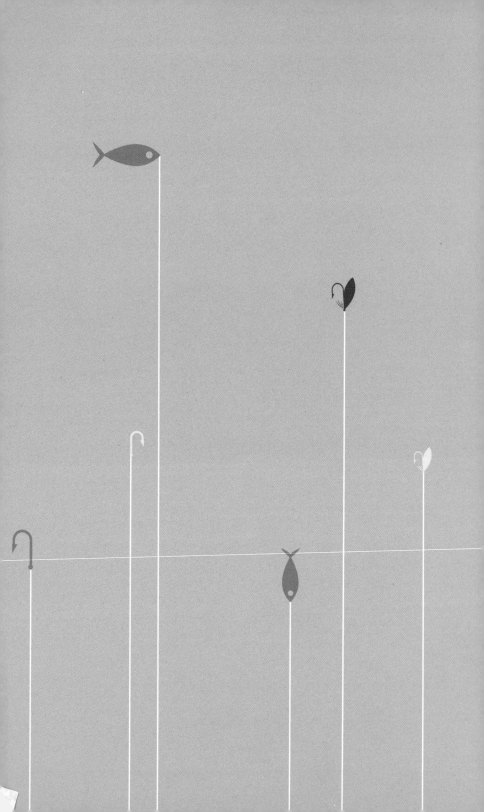